WADING BIRDS

by Anne Welsbacher

photographs by John Netherton

Pull Ahead Books

Lerner Publications Company • Minneapolis

Website address: www.lernerbooks.com

Curriculum Development Director: Nancy M. Campbell

Words in *italic type* are explained in a glossary
on page 30.

Library of Congress Cataloging-in-Publication Data

Welsbacher, Anne, 1955–
    Wading birds / by Anne Welsbacher ;
photographs by John Netherton.
        p.   cm. — (Pull ahead books)
    ˙Includes index.
    Summary: Describes the physical characteristics,
behavior, and habitat of North American wading birds.
        ISBN 0-8225-3614-5 (hardcover : alk. paper). —
        ISBN 0-8225-3620-X (paperback : alk. paper)
        1. Ciconiiformes—Juvenile literature. [1. Wading birds.
    2. Birds.] I. Netherton, John, ill. II. Title. III. Series.
    QL696.C5W45 1999
    598.3'4—dc21   98–18398

Manufactured in the United States of America
1 2 3 4 5 6 – JR – 04 03 02 01 00 99

Look at this great egret.
It has very long legs.

Why do you think its legs
are so long?

Great egrets are wading birds.

Wading birds walk in water
to look for food.

All wading birds have long legs,
long necks, and long beaks.

Long legs keep their bodies
high and dry above the water.

Long necks and beaks help the birds reach down to catch food.

Wading birds eat fish, frogs, bugs, snakes, and other small animals.

What is this reddish egret doing?

It is running in zigzags,
scaring up fish to eat.

This little blue heron is waiting
quietly for a fish to swim nearby.

Then it will stab at the fish
with its long beak!

Some birds hunt by walking with their beaks underwater.

This bird is called a *roseate* spoonbill. Can you guess why?

A roseate spoonbill's feathers
are pink like a rose.

Its beak,
which is
also called
a *bill,* is
shaped like
a spoon.

Many wading birds are named after the color of their feathers.

This is a yellow-crowned night-heron. Can you find its crown of feathers?

This is a green-backed heron.

Can you see
the green in
its feathers?

To keep its feathers pretty,
a wading bird *preens* them.

When a wading bird preens,
it rubs its feathers with its beak.

Preening
keeps the
feathers
waterproof,
neat, and
clean.

Some wading birds grow long, lacy feathers called *plumes.*

Plumes often grow when a bird is ready to raise a family.

These snowy egrets have plumes
on their backs.

Why is this bird
stretching its neck up?

Stretching
shows that
it wants to
find a *mate*
and raise
a family.

When a male wading bird finds
a mate, he brings her twigs.

The female takes the twigs
and builds a nest with them.

Wading birds usually build nests close together in big groups.

The nests are often high up in trees or bushes. Do you know why?

Some animals, like alligators,
eat birds.

Those hungry animals
cannot reach high nests.

When a female is finished building her nest, she lays eggs in it.

The eggs *hatch* three or four weeks later.

Out come chicks covered with fuzzy little feathers.

Soon the chicks grow
longer feathers.

Chicks are hungry. SQUAWK!
They call to their parents for food.

A parent brings food. The chick pulls down its parent's beak.

Then the parent throws up food into the chick's mouth.

Wading bird
chicks are
grown-up
in about
three
months.

Now each grown-up chick
must wade and hunt for itself!

Its long legs, neck, and
beak will help it survive.

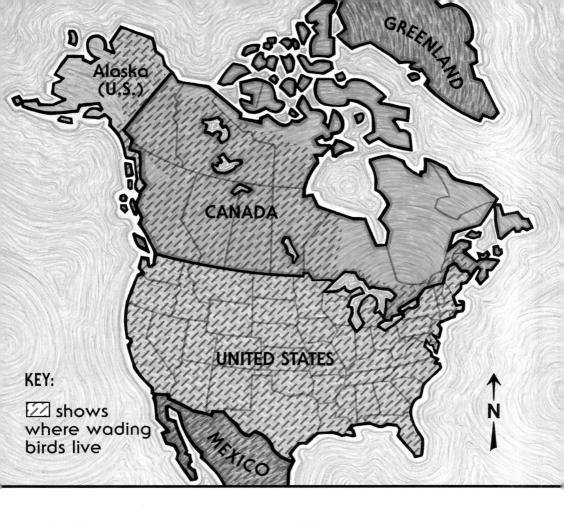

KEY:

⬚ shows
where wading
birds live

N

Find your state or province on this map.
Do wading birds live near you?

Parts of a Wading Bird's Body

wing

head

eye

neck

beak

feather

plume

tail

foot

leg

Glossary

bill: the hard mouth or beak of a bird

hatch: break open when the baby animals inside come out

mate: partner for raising a family

plumes: long, lacy feathers

preens: keeps feathers clean, neat, and waterproof. A wading bird preens its feathers by rubbing them with its beak.

roseate: pink like a rose

Hunt and Find

- wading birds **building nests** on pages 18–19
- **chicks** on pages 23–25
- **eggs** on page 22
- a wading bird **flying** on page 27
- wading birds **hunting** on pages 3–9
- **plumes** on pages 15–17

The publisher wishes to extend special thanks to our **series consultant,** Sharyn Fenwick. An elementary science-math specialist, Mrs. Fenwick was the recipient of the National Science Teachers Association 1991 Distinguished Teaching Award. In 1992, representing the state of Minnesota at the elementary level, she received the Presidential Award for Excellence in Math and Science Teaching.

About the Author

Edward Clark

Anne Welsbacher lives in Minnesota with her husband Edward, her stepdaughter Zoë, her dog, and two cats. She writes about animals, science, art, and health for magazines and newspapers. She is the author of more than 25 children's books about the stars, the history of the United States, and other topics. She also writes plays and enjoys listening to music. Anne watches eagles and other birds fly over the Mississippi River.

About the Photographer

Brenda Campbell

John Netherton has been a nature photographer for more than 30 years. He has taught and traveled throughout the United States and in many other countries. His work has been published in hundreds of books and magazines. Through these he shares his respect for nature and his commitment to recording it carefully. John has provided photos for four books in Lerner's Pull Ahead series. He lives in Nashville, Tennessee, and is the father of three sons: Jason, Joshua, and Erich.